What's So Funny About Business?

Yuppies, Bosses and Other Capitalists

William Kaufmann, Inc.

Los Altos, California

Library of Congress Cataloging-in-Publication Data
Harris, Sidney.
    What's so funny about business?

    Includes humorous introduction by the author posing
as Alexander Hamilton.
    1. Business ethics—Caricatures and cartoons.
2. American wit and humor, Pictorial.   I. Title.
HC1429.H33315A4   1986   741.5'973   86-21160

ISBN 0-86576-100-0

Printed in the United States of America

Introduction

Do you think there have always been as many cartoons in this country as there are today? Now they appear everywhere, but there was a time when we had no government and no cartoons.

Ben Franklin, that old entrepreneur, statesman, gadfly, ladies man, and curmudgeon, claimed he was responsible for the drawing of the rattlesnake that appears above the legend ''Don't tread on me,'' (but how can you believe anyone who also claims he discovered lightning?).

DON'T TREAD ON ME

This depiction became known in the Colonies as one of our first cartoons. Another one, published by big Ben in his *Pennsylvania Gazette* on May 9, 1754 (the year before I was born) looked like this:

J O I N, or D I E.

Would you believe (it is not common knowledge) that these were almost the only cartoons in the Colonies—which you now know as the United States of America—for almost 50 years? Regardless of how good those cartoons really were, two generations of this nation could only be expected to go so far on so little. So, while I was urging my fellow founding fathers to set up a national bank and issue paper money—and I assure you this was not done merely with a desire to see myself in my best suit on your modern $10 bill (although, in truth, I do admire the likeness)—I was also fighting vigorously to get the fledgling government of this country to provide funds for a few more cartoons. But Madison (or was it Monroe? I never could tell those two apart) had no sense of humor and argued that there was no rhyme or reason to justify additional cartoons for our people. He defended this firm position by repeatedly stating that the Constitution had not provided for any such frivolity. Monroe (or was it Madison?) agreed wholeheartedly.

Events too complex to summarize here gradually led to a proliferation of cartoons which now have virtually inundated this whole vast country. A handful of cartoons then were certainly too few, but now there are more cartoons in circulation than anyone needs, even if one is looking for some lighter fare than those Federalist Papers (of which I wrote a great part and which even today can be read with profit and will help you understand the U.S. Constitution). What this country *has* needed badly for some time, however, is a good collection of cartoons about modern business and related examples of bizarre behavior. Thus I am pleased to introduce this collection, which I recommend for your perusal.

Having been in positions of authority for much of my life (which was prematurely ended, as everyone knows, by that dastard, Aaron Burr), I particularly enjoy the way this cartoonist, S. Harris, draws people of executive standing—from the man at a party who is unhappy because there is no opportunity to sit down and vote for something, to the over-worked fellow who brings home a weekend-full of work (as well as the office pet, a guinea pig). And when I discovered that Orville Wright's luggage was lost after his historic 12-second flight, I recalled all of those portmanteaux of mine that went flying off stagecoaches I rode on those rocky roads through Upstate New York (where they later named a college[1] after me). Some of my bags may still be lying there, although they have probably been paved over by a thruway or parking lot. And I can certainly admire the man whose ingenious tax lawyer set him up as a holy man in Kashmir. Had there been income tax laws in 1780, heaven only knows what evasive moves I and some of my equally ingenious contemporaries might have been able to make. This cartoon from 1765 shows what we thought of taxes in general:

A common thread running through S. Harris's cartoons is the notion that the seemingly important and authoritarian forces in any society are full of flaws. Of course I knew that from observing John Adams and my other contemporary associates up close. I can assure those of you who weren't around in Adams' time that various traits of his are made abundantly clear in several of these cartoons. One drawing portrays a couple of people from a quality control department who admit they have no quality and no control, while another depicts a board of directors who are at a meeting not to *discuss* the company picnic but are about to *have* the company picnic right there at the table. That's economizing of a kind that I know a great deal about. When I became the first Secretary of the Treasury, the furnishings in my office cost about $10. You can thus realize how hard it is for me to grasp the concept in the cartoon showing a man with $643 million in his briefcase who shows up to discuss a corporate takeover. Our $66 million war debt after the American Revolution was an astronomical amount to us, but now I suppose it would be termed "a mere $66 million."

There are 120 cartoons in this volume, and many of them comment on situations I would never have dreamed of—then or now. Even Madison (or is it Monroe?) would have enjoyed this book, and I am certain you will, too.

On a personal note, I must mention how grateful I am to this country for keeping my memory alive, and I have often been asked which memorial most pleases me. The honor would go to Brooklyn for the complex accolade of naming a fort after me, and then naming a parkway after the fort.[2]

Alexander Hamilton

---

(1) And a most excellent college it remains to this day. "Mr. Hamilton consents to be a Trustee of the said Seminary; and will afford it all the aid in his power," noted a journal written early in 1793. Although a wood bust of Mr. Hamilton that once adorned a campus building named for him went up in flames more than a century ago, a fine bronze statue still proudly stands guard on the spacious lawn in front of the historic college chapel.—Ed.

(2) Fort Hamilton and Fort Hamilton Parkway.—Ibid.

"*Stop complaining. You knew what you were getting into when your father left you the business.*"

"You know the lifestyle so many of us dream about—living in a cabin in the woods, doing some pottery, perhaps weaving a wall hanging and selling it for just enough to buy a week's food, informal meals cooked in a fireplace, no pressure—well, I had enough of that and decided to drop out and become a business executive."

*"We may have a peer or two, but we definitely do **not** have a peer group."*

*"Don't we have **anyone** who took business administration?"*

"Given the downward slope of our demand curve and the ease with which other firms can enter the industry, we can strengthen our profit position only by equating marginal cost and marginal revenue. Order more jelly beans."

*"How the devil did all **this** go down 7³/₈ today?"*

"First thing we do is cut down on our executive-training program."

"Kickbacks, embezzlement, price fixing, bribery . . . this is an extremely high-crime area."

"We'll continue this tomorrow. I'm on a work-release program and I have to be back in my cell by six o'clock."

"Mr. Cummings will now discuss that gray area between legal acts and illegal acts."

"Oh, yeah! I'm a hell of a lot further beyond reproach than you are!"

"It has to be understandable, Higbe. A code of ethics is not actually to be written in code."

"All right—who stole my gavel?"

"You've been to business meetings and business lunches—believe me, you'll get used to business jogs."

*"This is the Businessman's Lunch—I ordered the **Tycoon's** Lunch!"*

"*This résumé is one of the most boastful, deceptive pieces of fraud I've ever seen. You're hired.*"

"It's not fair. You have classes and pep talks on selling, and I have to resist all on my own."

"It won't bother us if we're not allowed to aim our ads at the kids. The adults are easier to fool anyway."

"It appeals to greed, lust, pride, sloth and envy, but we're overlooking gluttony and avarice."

*"Why, he's referring to **us** as 'Brand X'!"*

"I prefer Brand X myself."

Dear Company:
I'm not interested in your product.

Signed,
Occupant

"Maybe the stuff stinks."

"*We're just not reaching the group between young marrieds and senior citizens.*"

"Let's face it—we have no quality and we have no control."

"It has been brought to my attention that some of us are not working at maximum efficiency . . ."

". . . No, he can't really fly . . . No, the bad guys don't really have a ray gun . . . No, this cereal really isn't the best food in the whole world . . . No, it won't make you as strong as a giant . . ."

"This restores my faith in America. Over two million box tops sent in, and only 37 box bottoms."

"Mr. Walter K. Flagg, Apex Corp., Detroit, Michigan, U.S.A. Dear Mr. Flagg: We are always very nice hearing from you. Your delighted letter, which we receiving of you . . . Pile it on thick. They really eat up this broken English . . ."

"Mr. Gottlieb recently read one of those books on Japanese management techniques."

"I'm sorry, but there's no room at the top, and there's no room in the middle, but there's a little room at the bottom."

*"I don't **enjoy** being an unreasonable tyrant, Gregg, but it **works**."*

"Your work is fine, and your attitude seems satisfactory, but I understand that after 15 years with us, you still haven't learned the company song."

"It's one of those days. Now Pritchard's pants have been recalled."

"We're all right as long as they think
we're talking millions."

*"I have to write a few reports, draw up some contracts,
and take care of the office guinea pig over the weekend."*

*"Haven't you heard? We're not going to **discuss** the company picnic—this **is** the company picnic."*

"Hello, dear. I had a very hard day at the office, and grabbed a bite on the way home. I've brought home some work, which I'll be doing in my study. See you in the morning. Good night."

"Directives from the Government, meetings with the Union, disputes with suppliers—it's getting more and more difficult to make bubble gum these days."

"The masked man? He's the Loan Arranger."

"Before we discuss our short-term interest rates, perhaps you could let me know how many hours you'll need the money for."

"I admire their frankness."

"This is not exactly my kind of gathering. What I like is when everyone sits around the table, each person airs his views, and then we vote."

"That's three 'Ayes,' two 'Nays,' one abstention, and one 'Go jump in the lake'."

"I have heard rumors that some of you find these meetings boring and dull. To counteract this, I have purchased a quantity of one-liners, which I shall interject from time to time."

"All those in favor . . ."

"The trouble with a merger like this is that our people who
know computers don't know a thing about bubble gum,
the people who know bubble gum don't know a thing
about hats, the people who know hats . . ."

"What bothers me about these meetings is even though it's work, I have the nagging feeling I ought to leave and get back to work."

"There's a gentleman out here with $643 million. He would like to discuss a takeover."

"It appears that Megalamp Industries, a conglomerate, wants to take over our family."

"Here's something you didn't count on—83,000 shares of the company stock up my sleeve!"

"Son, the Marshak Co. has taken us over, lock, stock and barrel. And old man Marshak—he's adopted you."

"It's not surprising. The production department is in Spain, the warehouse is in Korea, the accounting division is in Bolivia, the board of directors is in Canada . . ."

"I realized there was no store in the neighborhood where you could buy a book and you could also buy a pot."

SEARS & MELVILLE

GENERAL MERCHANDISE
AND
NOVELS

FAILED ALLIANCE

"This is your captain speaking. Transatlantic Airways has just been absorbed by Aero Argentina. Thus, instead of landing in London, we will touch down in Buenos Aires."

Immediately after Orville Wright's historic 12-second flight, his luggage could not be located.

"It doesn't look good. Some of our nationals are at war with some of our other nationals."

*"We've received a rather large order from the State of New Jersey.
Try to find out why the State of New Jersey needs 55 jet fighter planes."*

"Our stock has been going up all week. What are we doing right?"

"Billy, I want to interest you in our new Kandy Kredit Kard."

*"You know Daddy has a very important job and he has to
be very careful. Now sit down and put on your I.D. card."*

"He may have a Ph.D. in elementary particle physics, but he's having an awful lot of trouble with the application form."

"According to today's boxscore, Rackley, you've made a couple of errors and you didn't score any runs."

"A ground ball to deep short, handled beautifully by Santana—he should be able to renegotiate his contract on that—the throw to first is high, Hernandez pulls it down—putting him in a real strong bargaining position as a free agent. Garvey, now 0 for 3, is weakening his post season options considerably . . ."

"Talk to my lawyer."

"*I'm so proud to be part of a profession that has never discriminated against women.*"

"Once you do transmute lead into gold, you'll find the market for it is very speculative."

"I've been out here a long time. Is it still $35 an ounce?"

"*I didn't ask you to help me when it was $90 an ounce, and I didn't ask you to help me when it was $110 an ounce. But when it's $400 an ounce . . .*"

*"Don't be discouraged. **Gravel** is $3 an ounce."*

*"What bothers me is that we all **look** so successful."*

"What it comes down to is our software is
too hard and our hardware is too soft."

"All right, profits are down, but look at all the things that are up."

"One thing is certain. It's not just a seasonal slump."

*"But look on the bright side. We did not create
even one single hazardous waste!"*

S. Harris

"It's a miracle the way he keeps his desk so clean."

"Mr. Labine is not at his desk at the moment."

"I think Willis has gone overboard with his 'agribusiness' image."

"I got where I am by economizing wherever possible. For example, I still make and receive my phone calls at the luncheonette downstairs."

*"How come **your** hard days at the office are harder than anyone else's hard days at the office?"*

"You'll have to decide—do you want to be top management in a small pond, or bottom management in a big pond?"

"I fired them all. 2,437 of them. I'll go it alone."

"*James Waterstone III, Chairman and Chief Executive Officer, Fairtex Industries. Dear Jamie: Thank you very much for the lovely towels you sent me for my birthday. Yours truly, V. Farnsworth Bridgely.*"

"Inspectors, Robinson, do not express opinions."

"With a five-day week I golfed and fished. On a four-day week I took up bowling, and with the three-day week I started skiing. Gentlemen, I'm too tired for a two-day week."

"I have the result of your cost-benefit analysis. You should have retired four years ago."

"Interesting résumé, but what have you done lately?"

"We have something with terrific fringe benefits.
No salary—just fringe benefits."

"This is not the kind of perk I had in mind."

"Another setback—the mediators just went out on strike."

"After two days of mediating, it turned out that the telephone company executives were negotiating with the union from Westinghouse."

*"Send it back to committee—oh—this **is** committee."*

"Then it's settled. We'll make 7 million with blue handles, 5 million with red handles, 4 million with purple handles and 2 million with green handles."

"Let's try to make this an interesting meeting. My biographer will be here."

"Then go ahead with the merger."
"Make them the offer we discussed."
"How many shares are outstanding?"

"Pineapple will be fine."
"All right dear, then vegetable soup."
"Of course they'll like vegetable soup . . ."

*"Let's get this straight. The business runs itself. You go to a board meeting once a month. What do you want to retire **from?**"*

"Kicking you upstairs is, of course, just a figure of speech. What we're really doing is sending you deeper into the countryside."

"You must realize that desire is the cause of almost all unhappiness—but, just out of curiosity, where could I get a suit like that?"

"I've found enlightenment, and I still pull down my
$250,000 per. What more can I ask?"

*"How could the government possibly afford a guaranteed annual income? As I see it, the average family needs at **least** $125,000 per year."*

"Keep it. I'm an eccentric millionaire myself."

"Last week I'm running an electronics plant in Ohio—today I'm a holy man in Kashmir. What won't my tax lawyer think of next?"

"It would be better than tribute, better than plunder. You could make a veritable fortune if you'd let this go condo."

What's So Funny about Science?

Cartoons by **Sidney Harris**
From **American Scientist**
Foreword by **Herbert S. Bailey, Jr.**

"There's a lot to laugh about in science and a lot that can be made fun of."
— *Current Contents*

"Scientists have a hard time taking humor seriously."
— *The New York Times Magazine*

S. Harris likes science and knows its importance. But he also thinks a lot of things about science are funny, including the scientists themselves. By his wonderful imagination and inspired pen he shows how funny human animals — and other animals — sometimes are, and how even dreadful matters like pollution and nuclear dangers have their humorous aspects.
Cartoons by S. Harris have appeared regularly in *American Scientist* since January 1970.

WHAT'S SO FUNNY ABOUT COMPUTERS?

cartoons by S. Harris

For all those hopelessly or happily entangled in computer circuitry, Sidney Harris will help them unwind with *What's So Funny about Computers?*, a book of cartoons sure to prompt snickers, guffaws, chortles, and even outright belly-laughs. Both computer jocks and victims of "terminal shock" (the most mysterious, baffling, and unfathomable malady to afflict this Computer Age) will see themselves reflected in the more than 100 drawings in Harris's latest book. But what's the best thing about these engaging and witty computer cartoons? There's always some byte to them.

"THIS USED TO TAKE HOURS."

ISBN 0-86576-049-7

ALL ENDS UP

by **S. Harris**
Foreword by **Dr. Linus Pauling**

All Ends Up is the third collection of S. Harris cartoons published by William Kaufmann, Inc. After reading the first in the trio, *What's So Funny About Science?*, Isaac Asimov commented: "What's so funny about science? Sidney Harris, that's what." In his Foreword to the second collection, *Chicken Soup and Other Medical Matters*, Willard Espy observed that "a great cartoonist like Sidney Harris makes even mortality hilarious." And in response to the same book, Abby Van Buren wrote, "What this world needs right now is a good laugh. *Chicken Soup* provides at least 100!"
You will find a profusion of new laughs (more than 120, in fact) waiting for you inside *All Ends Up*.

"This is the part I always hate."

ISBN: 086576-000-4

CHICKEN SOUP

and other medical matters

by

S. Harris

Foreword by
Willard R. Espy

ISBN 0-913232-74-2